HOW DID WE FIND OUT ABOUT
LIFE IN THE DEEP SEA?

HOW DID WE FIND OUT ABOUT

LIFE IN THE DEEP SEA?

Isaac Asimov
Illustrated by David Wool

WALKER AND COMPANY
New York

Library of Congress Cataloging in Publication Data

Asimov, Issac, 1920–
  How did we find out about life in the deep sea?

  Includes index.
  Summary: Describes the discovery of life in the
deep oceans and explains oceanography.
    1. Marine biology—Juvenile literature.
2. Oceanography—Juvenile literature. [1. Marine
biology. 2. Oceanography] I. Title.
QH91.16.A84   1981   574.92   81-13141
ISBN 0-8027-6427-4   AACR2
ISBN 0-8027-6428-2 (lib. bdg.)

First published in the United States of America
in 1981 by the Walker Publishing Company, Inc.

Published simultaneously in Canada by John Wiley & Sons Canada,
Limited, Rexdale, Ontario.

ISBN: 0-8027-6427-4 Tr.
      0-8027-6428-2 Reinf.

Library of Congress Catalog Card Number: 81-50732

Printed in the United States of America

10 9 8 7 6 5 4 3 2 1

To
Robyn Joan Asimov, B.A., M.S.W.

Contents

THE EARTH FROM SPACE

1 Life in the Ocean Surface

ABOUT 70 PERCENT of the earth's surface is covered by the ocean. The continents are large islands set in that ocean, and all the dry land in the whole world makes up considerably less than half the area of the ocean.

All we see is the top of the ocean.

If you look through a glass of water, it seems transparent. Light passes through it easily.

You can see to the bottom of a brook, if the water is clear, or even to the bottom of a pond. You cannot see to the bottom of a large river or lake, and you certainly can't see through the water of the ocean. This is because light is absorbed, little by little, as it passes through thicker and thicker layers of water.

The result is that through most of history human beings knew nothing about what was under the top layer of the ocean. They didn't even have any idea of how deep the ocean might be, or whether there was any bottom to it at all.

People knew there were living creatures in rivers and lakes, of course, and in the ocean, too. There were fish of various kinds. There were also shellfish, such as oysters, clams, and lobsters. Even prehistoric people used to fish for food, and in some places living things from the sea made up a very important part of the food supply.

Did any of those very early fishermen ever wonder how far down in the ocean fish and other creatures could be found? Some may have supposed there were fish all the way down to the bottom, but how could anyone ever find out?

Of course, one could dive down into the water, but you can't dive very deep, and you can't stay down there very long.

In some places there are trained divers who make their way downward to where special kinds of oysters live attached to rocks. In those oysters pearls are sometimes found.

Since pearls are very valuable, people make enormous efforts to get them. Divers can kick their way downward to a depth of 50 feet or so and may then spend a minute and a half under water, gathering all the oysters they can before their breath begins to run out.

Such divers could tell that life existed in great quantity down to 50 feet below the surface, but what about still greater depths?

By the year 1800 people thought they had an answer to the question. They were sure, even

PEARL DIVER

9

without looking, that there couldn't be any life far below the topmost layer of the ocean. This is the way they worked that out.

All animal life depends on plant life for food. Some animals live on other animals, but those other animals eat plants. No matter how long a chain you may have of animals that eat animals that eat animals that eat animals and so on, eventually you come to animals that eat plants.

If plants suddenly disappeared, then animals that live on plants would starve to death. Animals that live on *those* animals would then starve to death. Eventually there would be no animals at all.

What keeps the plants going? Why don't they all get eaten up? Plants keep growing by building new tissues (stems, leaves, roots) out of carbon dioxide from the air, water from the soil, and certain chemicals in the water.

It takes energy to put those substances together, and the energy comes from sunlight. If there were no sunlight, plants could not grow. After animals had eaten up all the existing plants, there would be no more and the animals would starve. If the sun stopped shining, life on earth would disappear after a while. But as long as the sun shines, plants continue to grow and animals continue to live.

It's the same way in the sea. In the uppermost layers of the sea there are countless billions of tiny plants so small that they can only be seen through a microscope.

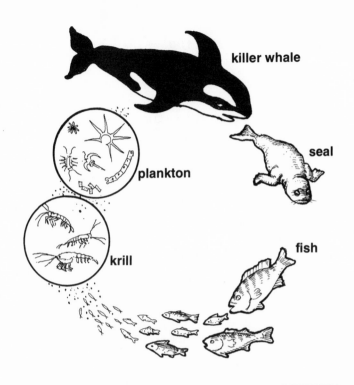

OCEAN FOOD CHAIN STARTS WITH PLANKTON

Tiny animals live on those tiny plants; slightly larger animals live on the tiny animals; still larger animals live on the smaller ones; and so on. Without those tiny plants to begin with, all the animals would die. And the plants themselves couldn't keep growing without sunlight.

Sunlight, however, doesn't penetrate very far into the water. It reaches only about 250 feet down from the surface in sufficient quantity to keep those tiny plants growing. The top 250 feet of the ocean is therefore called the *euphotic zone* (yoo-FOH-tik, from Greek words meaning "good light").

By 1800 scientists knew that plants need light to live, and to them it meant that below the 250-foot-thick euphotic zone, there were no growing plants. Nowadays we know that the average depth of the ocean is about 12,400 feet (2⅓ miles). The euphotic zone makes up only 2 percent of the ocean.

Animals might swim downward out of the euphotic zone, the scientists thought, but they couldn't get too far away from the basic food supply of all life. Therefore, it seemed to scientists in 1800, all life in the sea had to be in and slightly below the euphotic zone. The deeper parts of the ocean had to be lifeless.

Of course, scientists were interested in finding out all they could about life in the upper layers, but diving wasn't the answer. Even if scientists were willing to dive into the water, they couldn't stay down there long enough to do their studies.

Instead of going down to see the ocean life, they began to think of ways of bringing ocean life up to the surface. In the 1770s, for instance, a Danish biologist, Otto F. Müller (MYOO-ler, 1730–1784), made a special dredge for himself. It was a strong net attached to an iron frame, and it could be trailed many feet below the water. Living things would be tangled in the mesh and would be brought up.

One person who used a dredge successfully was an English biologist, Edward Forbes, Jr.

EDWARD FORBES

(1815–1854). He wrote a poem about his dredge in 1839, which goes as follows:

> *Down in the deep, where the mermen sleep,*
> *Our gallant dredge is sinking;*
> *Each finny shape in a precious scrape*
> *Will find itself in a twinkling!*
>
> *They may twirl and twist, and writhe as they*
>   *wist,*
> *And break themselves into sections,*
> *But up they all, at the dredge's call,*
> *Must come to fill collections.*

During the 1830s Forbes dredged up sea life from the North Sea and other waters around the British Isles. Then, in 1841, he joined a naval ship that was going to the eastern Mediterranean, and there he did more and better dredging than anyone had yet done, studying all the kinds of living things he brought up. He found life well below the euphotic zone. He dredged up a starfish from a depth of a quarter of a mile, for instance.

DREDGE USED BY FORBES

Forbes wrote scientific papers in which he described the kinds of living things that existed in the different parts of the ocean that he had dredged. He showed that different varieties, or *species* (SPEE-sheez), of plants and animals can be found in different parts of the ocean, just as they can be found in different places on land.

He showed, too, that different species of living things can be found at different depths in the sea.

Forbes found life to depths of 1,800 feet below the surface (⅓ mile), but that, he felt, was the limit. In a book he published in 1843 he suggested that at depths lower than 1,800 feet there was probably no life at all.

He called the region below that limit the *azoic* (uh-ZOH-ik) region, from Greek words meaning "no life." If Forbes were right, this would mean that 85 percent of the ocean was completely lifeless.

2 Cables and Currents

EVEN AS Forbes was deciding that the ocean was largely lifeless, his limit of 1,800 feet was being broken.

By the 1840s explorers were aware that in the South Polar regions there was an icy continent on which no human beings had ever set foot.*

One of the explorers who took his ships down to the rim of that continent was an Englishman, James Clark Ross (1800–1862). In 1841 he located a large gulf in the continent of Antarctica, a gulf that has ever since been called Ross Sea.

Ross wasn't satisfied just to follow the shape of the coastline of the mysterious land at the South Pole. He tried to find out everything he could about the ocean around it.

How Did We Find Out About Antarctica (New York: Walker, 1980).

16

JAMES CLARK ROSS

In fact, he was the first one to try to determine how deep the ocean might be. He let down a long cable with a weight at the end of it, hoping to hit bottom. He also used dredges farther down than anyone ever had before and brought up all sorts of sea life from a depth of 2,400 feet. That's nearly half a mile deep, considerably deeper than the depth Forbes was considering to be the limit of life.

Somehow, Ross's findings didn't make much of an impression. For one thing, it happened far, far away from Europe, so European scientists found it easy to ignore it. Besides, they were so sure that life couldn't exist so far down below the euphotic zone that they just paid no attention to anything that showed the contrary.

By that time, though, people had become interested in the deep sea for reasons that had nothing to do with life.

In 1844 an American inventor, Samuel F. B. Morse (1791–1872) had constructed the first telegraph line. It ran from Baltimore, Maryland, to Washington, D.C., a distance of 40 miles.

For the first time, signals could be sent long distances in a tiny fraction of a second. Soon telegraph lines were strung along poles all over the United States and other countries.

Some places are separated by water, however. You can't very well place poles in the water and string wires on them. But you could wrap the wires in waterproof coatings and make cables out of them. The cables could then be laid along the bottom of a stretch of water. Cables were laid across the bottom of the Hudson River and of the Mississippi River in the 1840s, for instance.

In the 1850s, cables were laid across the English Channel and the Irish Sea. That connected England, by telegraph, with Ireland and France.

The big job, however, was to stretch a cable across 3,000 miles of the Atlantic Ocean, in order to connect Europe and North America.

SAMUEL F.B. MORSE

This could be very important. For example, in December 1814 Great Britain and the United States had signed a treaty of peace in Ghent, Belgium, that ended the War of 1812. News of the treaty, however, couldn't reach the United States until a ship traveled across the Atlantic Ocean with the information—and that took 6 weeks. Before the ship reached the United States, the Battle of New Orleans was fought on January 8, 1815. It was the largest and bloodiest battle of the war, and it was fought when the war was supposed to be over.

Once a cable was laid across the Atlantic Ocean, nothing like that could ever happen again.

In order to lay such a cable successfully, something had to be known about the ocean floor. How deep was it? How level was it? People had to carry on the task begun by Ross. They had to lower weighted lines in order to try to reach the ocean bottom. This was called *sounding*.

In 1860 the British ship, *Bulldog* set sail across the Atlantic Ocean, hoping to make a number of soundings that would help make an Atlantic Cable a success. (A couple of attempts to lay the cable, in 1857 and in 1858, had already failed.)

On board the *Bulldog* was a British doctor named George C. Wallich (1815–1899), who was in charge of any discoveries that might be made about sea life. He was watching in October, when a line was heaved overboard at a spot in the Atlantic Ocean about halfway between the northern tip of Scotland and the southern tip of Greenland.

The sounding line went down to a depth of 7,560 feet, or nearly 1½ miles. When the line was brought up, thirteen starfish were found near the lower end of it. What's more, they were not starfish that had died and sunk to the sea bottom. The starfish were very much alive.

Wallich reported this at once and insisted that animal life could exist in the cold darkness of the deep sea, even without plants.

DEEP-SEA STARFISH

Again scientists ignored the matter. It was just an isolated incident that didn't seem to fit in with what they thought they knew, and it was easier to look the other way.

Not everyone looked the other way, though. There was one exception, a Scottish biologist, Charles W. Thomson (1830–1882). He was interested in sea life, and he wanted to settle the matter of life below Forbes's limits once and for all.

He had a friend who was vice-president of the Royal Society, which was the most important scientific organization in Great Britain. Together they managed to get the Royal Society to put up the money for a scientific expedition to study the deep sea.

In 1868 Thomson went out into the North Atlantic on a ship called *Lightning*.

He did indeed settle the matter. Dredging below Forbes's 1,800-foot mark, he obtained ani-

CHARLES W. THOMPSON

mals of all kinds, and all argument ended. Forbes's idea of a lower limit of life vanished.

Thomson made a particularly important discovery when he measured the temperature of water at different depths.

It had been thought till then that all the water in the deeper layers of the sea had the same temperature—4° Celsius (39° Fahrenheit).

At 4° C. water is at its densest. A particular quantity of water at this temperature is heavier than the same quantity of water at temperatures that are either higher or lower. Water at 4° C. should therefore sink to the bottom and lie there.

Thomson showed, however, that water at a given depth in different places varies in temperature. In some places, it is quite a bit warmer than 4° C.

Where does the warmer water come from? It didn't seem that the sea bottom could be a source of heat. At least, there was no sign of such heat. The water had to come from the upper layers, which are warmed by the sun. This meant there must be water currents that carry water from the surface of the ocean down into the depths. There must therefore be other currents that carry water from the depths to the surface.

OCEAN CURRENTS

——————warm current
------------cold current

Scientists had known all along that there are currents on the surface that carry surface water from the polar regions to the tropics and back. Now they knew there are currents that carry surface water to the bottom and back. Water circulates through the whole ocean, and that meant scientists could finally understand how life exists far below the euphotic zone.

The water in the ocean surface has dissolved oxygen from the air. Animal life in the sea lives on that dissolved oxygen. The ocean currents carry that dissolved oxygen all the way down to the very bottom, so living things can get the oxygen they need at any depth.

But how do deep-sea animals get food when there are no plants in the darkness down there?

What happens is this:

When an animal eats a plant or another animal, bits of the object being eaten may break off and drift downward. Sometimes plants or animals in the euphotic zone just die and drift downward.

As these once-living objects drift downward, they are seized and eaten by animals living at lower levels in the water. Those animals in the lower levels may be eaten, or they may die in other ways, so part of them or all of them sinks still farther downward.

There is a continuous drizzle of once-living matter that sinks all the way to the floor of the ocean. This drizzle supports small animals, which are eaten by large animals, which are eaten by still larger animals, and so on. Finally the drizzle reaches the bottom of the ocean.

At the bottom it is eaten by animals scurrying along the floor, or it is decomposed by bacteria that live there.

If that were all there were to it, then all the chemicals in the surface layers of water that support life would gradually be transferred to the ocean bottom. They would all concentrate at the bottom until there was nothing left at the surface. Life would then be impossible on the surface.

Since it is the surface plants that support life all through the ocean, partly by being eaten at the surface and partly by the drizzle downward, life in the ocean would stop altogether.

The material that reaches the bottom of the ocean, however, doesn't stay there. Remember the currents that carry water from the surface of the ocean to the bottom and back up again.

The currents coming up from below carry the chemicals that sank to the bottom. They reach the surface, and there the plant cells in the euphotic zone use them for growth. Tiny animals multiply as they eat the plant cells. The whole thing starts all over again.

Without the currents that keep mixing the waters of the ocean, from top to bottom and bottom to top, life couldn't exist anywhere on earth. Life began first in the sea, and only colonized the land billions of years later. Therefore, if life couldn't have existed in the sea, it could never have colonized the land, and life as we know it would not be here.

A small discovery, such as differences in temperature in deep layers of the sea can be very important.

DRIZZLE EFFECT

3 The *Challenger* Expedition

IN 1869 THOMSON went out in another ship, the *Porcupine*, and managed to dredge down to a distance of 2¾ miles and still come up with different species of animals. Thomson began to feel certain that life existed all the way down to the bottom of the ocean, however deep that might be.

But how deep was it? Thomson felt the need for a real investigation. He wanted an expedition that would go through all the oceans and investigate conditions in a variety of different places, not just in the regions near the British Isles.

This time he got support not only from the Royal Society but from the British Navy, which was the largest in the world. The British Navy controlled the seas, and Great Britain depended on her navy to support her growing empire—the largest the world had ever seen. The more the Navy knew about the ocean, the better it could do its job, so it felt it would be worth investing some money in Thomson's project.

Thomson set out on December 7, 1872, in a ship called *Challenger* and remained at sea for 3½ years. The *Challenger* sailed over all the oceans, traveling nearly 80,000 miles. The depth of the ocean was measured in 362 different places. In the Pacific Ocean, which turned out to be the deepest as well as the largest, there were places where bottom was reached 4½ miles down from the surface.

Even in the deepest part of the ocean that could be reached by the ship's sounding lines, living things were brought up.

S.S. CHALLENGER

The living things that were brought up were the same kind of animals that lived near the surface: fish, starfish, crayfish, clams, and so on. They were often different species from those that existed nearer the surface, but they were not totally different.

It was as though life had begun near the surface of the ocean and had gradually colonized the deeps, just as it had colonized the land. In moving down to the deeps, life evolved into somewhat different forms, just as it had on land, but these life forms clearly resembled the ones on land.

Thomson was knighted in 1876 for his services to science. He then set to work on a series of books that would describe all the findings of the *Challenger* expedition. It eventually appeared in many volumes, but Thomson did not live to see the completion of the job. He died only five days after his fifty-second birthday.

Thanks to Thomson, we now know that life exists in the deep sea, but the lower layers are not as full of life as the surface layers are. They can't be.

The animals near the bottom of the ocean have to depend upon a drizzle of food from the top, with all the animals helping themselves on its way down. The farther down you go, the thinner the drizzle and the fewer the number of living things. At the very bottom is the end of the line; the animals that are served last, so to speak.

Many of the deep-sea species of animals are of the kind that do not move around much: sponges, starfish, sea urchins, sea lilies, sea cucumbers, and so on. Moving around takes energy, and to have enough energy for motion you have to have a good-sized food supply, which you don't have at the bottom.

Just the same, there are some fish in the deep sea that do swim about, though rather slowly and weakly. The best-known fish of the deep sea are the *anglerfish*.

There are about 210 different species of anglerfish, and the largest are up to 4 feet long. Most are small, though.

The anglerfish are basically like the familiar

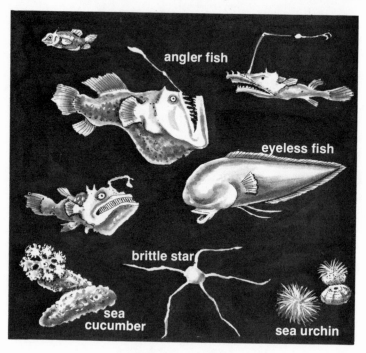

DEEP-SEA ANIMALS

fish we know, but they have some unusual features. For instance, some of them have luminous spots. There are a number of animal species that possess the ability to carry on chemical reactions that produce light in certain parts of the body. Think of the familiar firefly that glows in the gardens in the spring.

In the deep sea many animals can produce light on their bodies in particular patterns. This does not do much to light up surroundings that are otherwise pitch dark. The luminous spots produce very feeble light and don't really light up anything in the neighborhood.

The spots themselves can be seen, however, and they may enable the males and females of a particular species to see and recognize each other.

Some deep-sea fish have big eyes that detect feeble flashes of light. Others, which haven't developed luminous spots, have no eyes. They generally grope over the bottom of the sea, feeling for bits of food they can eat and for others like themselves with whom they can mate.

The most unusual thing about anglerfish is the first spine of the fin on the upper surface. This spine is detached from the fin and is located on the head of the anglerfish. At the end of the spine there is a fleshy growth that in some species looks and wiggles like a worm. In other species it may even look like a little fish. This growth is always luminous.

Other animals who see this growth react as though it might be a piece of food: They swim toward it. When they come close enough, the anglerfish opens its large mouth and swallows the animal. It is just as though the spine is a fishing rod and the luminous growth is bait. It is because the anglerfish uses a "rod and bait" to lure small animals toward its mouth that it is called the anglerfish.

In some anglerfish the female is much larger than the male. The male anglerfish, when it finds a young female, bites the abdomen of the female. It then remains there as long as the female lives. The blood streams of the two become connected, and the male has no independent existence after that. It becomes part of the female and does nothing more than fertilize any eggs she produces.

In this way, the anglerfish does not have to run much risk of not finding a mate in the dark. The male has to find a female just once, and after that nothing more needs to be done.

Every once in a while, a deep-sea fish has a chance to have a big meal. It comes across another

ANGLER FISH

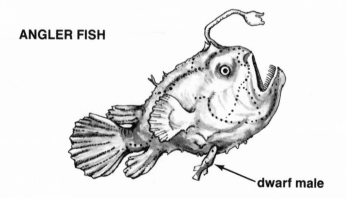

dwarf male

fish as large as itself; or else an unusually large piece of food comes drifting down from the upper regions. In either case it helps a fish to be ready to take advantage quickly.

There are some deep-sea fish called "gulpers," which specialize in this. They have long, thin bodies and tails, and some are as much as 6 feet long. At the front of these thin bodies is a huge head, which is almost all mouth. In some species of gulpers the head and mouth are longer than the rest of the body.

When a large object comes near one of these gulpers, that huge mouth opens and gulps. Down slides the food into a stomach that expands like a rubber balloon, and there the food is slowly digested. The gulper is one animal that can swallow another animal larger than itself.

One such meal can naturally last a gulper a long time.

GULPER FISH

before and after eating

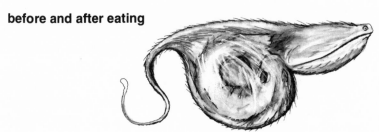

33

4 Squids and Coelacanths

ANIMALS SUCH as anglerfish and gulpers look grotesque, and their big mouths are frightening. However, they are usually small and slow and always stay far down in the ocean deep. They are no threat to human beings at all, and they never were.

There have always been tales of huge sea monsters, however.

To be sure, there are huge whales that are larger than any animals on land. It may have been such whales that first gave people the idea of sea monsters.

The largest of the whales is the blue whale. The largest blue whale of which there is any record had a length of 104 feet and may have weighed as much as 150 tons. A blue whale can weigh as much as fifteen large elephants, and weighs twice as much as the very largest dinosaur that ever lived.

In fact, it seems that the blue whale is the largest animal we know of that ever lived on the earth. Yet might there not be still larger animals living somewhere deep in the sea, animals that we have never been able to capture and study?

Monsters have indeed been occasionally reported. In Greek mythology, for example, there was the monstrous Hydra, slain by Hercules. It had nine necks, each one ending in a poisonous head. There was Scylla, who had six long necks ending in heads that yapped like puppies. There was Medusa, who had living snakes for hair.

Possibly all these monsters were inspired by large octopuses or jellyfish. These possess snake-like tentacles, which seem frightening to people who are used to land animals with ordinary legs.

A particularly large tentacled sea monster was reported by various Scandinavian writers. The most popular account was by Erik L. Pontoppidan (pon-TOP-ih-dahn, 1698–1764), who was the bishop of Bergen in Norway.

In 1752 he published a book called *A Natural History of Norway*, in which he described a monster he called the *kraken*. He described the kraken as having a round body about a mile and a half in circumference, with huge tentacles attached. This would make the kraken about 2,500 feet across, without counting the tentacles, and it would easily weigh as much as a thousand of the largest blue whales.

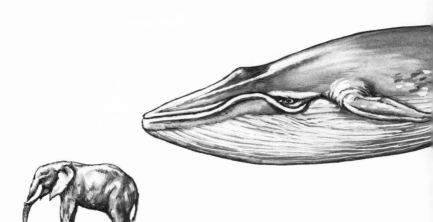

Pontoppidan described its tentacles as being able to wrap around the largest ships and being able to drag them under water.

A monster that size is hard to believe, and yet sperm whales were often found with large tentacles in their stomachs.

Blue whales and many other very large whales feed on tiny creatures. They open their huge mouths and take in hundreds of gallons of sea water which filters out through strips of "whalebone" that fringe their mouths. Small shrimp and fish remain behind and are swallowed.

Other whales have teeth, however, and can

seize and bite pieces off large animals. The
largest of these is the sperm whale. The sperm
whale sometimes reaches a length of as much as
67 feet long and weighs as much as 80 tons, about
half the size of a blue whale.

Could we imagine a sperm whale nipping a
piece off a kraken?

That seems unlikely. If a kraken were as large
as Bishop Pontoppidan said, the sperm whale
would be just a small mouthful to it. Perhaps, the
account of the kraken was exaggerated.

There are squids, animals related to the oc-
topus, that have longer heads, longer tentacles,

and are faster moving. The squids that were familiar to people were quite small, but every once in a while a giant squid was reported.

Such giant squids might live about half a mile deep in the ocean and might only appear at the surface on rare occasions. Sperm whales can dive half a mile deep and stay there for half an hour or so. Perhaps they do this in search of the giant squid.

In 1853 there was a report of a giant squid that had washed up on a beach in Denmark. It was cut up for fish bait before it could be examined by scientists.

There were other reports of this kind, and then, in 1861, a giant squid was actually harpooned and taken on board ship. By the 1870s there were many such cases reported, and scientists were ready to admit that the giant squid existed and that it probably formed the basis for the tales of the legendary kraken.

To be sure, even the largest giant squid is nothing like the kraken. The giant squids are the largest invertebrates (animals without an internal skeleton) known to have ever existed—at least as far as weight is concerned. (Some jellyfish are longer but are very light.)

Even the largest giant squids, however, are probably no more than 50 feet long, and most of that consists of its long tentacles. Even a large giant squid probably doesn't weigh more than 2 tons at most, which is not much more than half that of a hippopotamus.

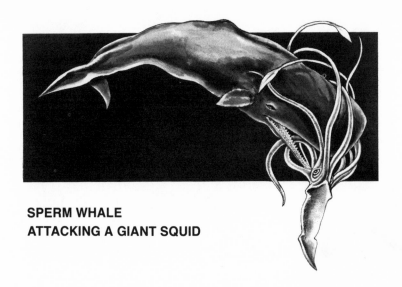

**SPERM WHALE
ATTACKING A GIANT SQUID**

The giant squid has the largest eye of any animal that ever lived, for its eyes are up to 15 inches across. Compare this with the eyes of a large blue whale, which are less than 5 inches across.

Are there animals larger than the giant squid, perhaps even larger than the blue whale, that live in some hidden part of the ocean? There are reports of sea serpents all the time, for instance, especially in the rather small Scottish lake of Loch Ness.

It seems unlikely that sea serpents, even if they exist, would be very large. The chances are that though some forms of sea life remain to be found, the blue whale's record as the largest of all animals will not be broken.

Record size, however, is not the only remarkable thing we might find.

On December 25, 1938, a ship, fishing off South Africa, brought up an odd fish about 5 feet long. Its fins were attached to fleshy lobes, instead of directly to the body.

The curator of a museum in London saw the fish when the ship got to port. She made a sketch of it and sent it to a scientist named James L. B. Smith (1897–1968.) He recognized it at once as a *coelacanth* (SEE-luh-kanth), a kind of fish that was well known but that had been thought to be extinct for 70 million years. This coelacanth died and was thrown away.

Smith advertised all over eastern Africa for fishermen to be on the watch for such a fish. He asked them to get in touch with him at once if they caught one. Unfortunately, World War II began a year later, and nothing could be done for years.

In December 1952, however, a second coelacanth was caught and, by 1970, a total of sixty had been obtained off the Comoro Islands, just

COELACANTH

northwest of Madagascar. Not only were these fish not extinct, but they weren't even particularly rare. But they lived at depths of nearly 1,000 feet and rarely approached the surface.

The coelacanths belonged to a group of fish that, about 300 million years ago, left the ocean and invaded the land. Scientists were particularly interested in studying them alive.

5 Mountains and Trenches

FOR ABOUT 50 years after the *Challenger* expedition, nothing much was done about the ocean deeps. After all, what could be done but to drop more sounding lines here and there? However, lowering a line that is miles long and then raising it again is a long and difficult job. Even after that had been done, it just gave you the depth at one point in the vast ocean.

Even if thousands of soundings were taken (which would take years and years), it would merely give you thousands of single points. You still wouldn't know what the ocean bottom was like between the points. There seemed no reason to try to learn more about the ocean depths unless you had some way that was better than dropping a line overboard.

Something turned up during World War I. A French physicist, Paul Langevin (lahnzh-VAN), 1872–1946), was trying to work out a way of detecting enemy submarines.

Langevin had studied under Pierre Curie (kyoo-REE, 1859–1906), another French physicist. Curie had discovered in 1880 that if a rapidly changing electric current was sent through a crystal, that crystal was made to vibrate very rapidly. This vibration set up sound waves in the air, but the sound waves were so short the human ear could not hear them. Such sound is called *ultrasonic* (UL-truh-SON-ik) vibrations.

Ordinary sound waves widen as they move and curve around obstacles. The tiny sound waves of ultrasonic vibrations, however, move much more nearly in a straight line and, when they hit an obstacle, they bounce back and are thus reflected.

Langevin thought he might make use of ultrasonic vibrations to detect submarines. A beam of such vibrations would be sent through the water. There they might strike a submarine and be reflected. The reflected beam would be detected, and the direction from which it returned would be the direction of the submarine. Since the speed of sound through water is known, the time it would take for the reflected sound to come back would tell how far away the submarine was.

Such a device would be used for navigation, since it would detect obstacles ahead, and for *ranging*, which means telling the distance of an obstacle. The device, then, can be described as

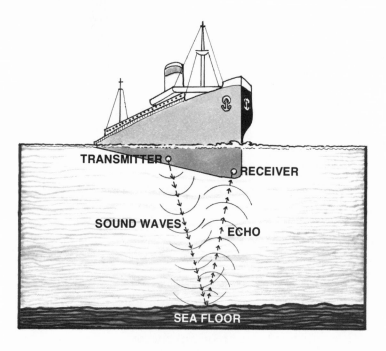

HOW SONAR WORKS

"*s*ound *n*avigation *a*nd *r*anging," which is abbreviated as *sonar* (SOH-nahr.)

By the time Langevin had this device perfected, World War I was over. As it happened, however, sonar could be used for peaceful purposes. If a beam of ultrasonic vibrations is sent downward into the oceans, it would reach the bottom and be reflected. By measuring the time it took the beam to return, one could calculate how far down the bottom was.

Instead of the long, tedious, difficult job of throwing sounding lines overboard and pulling them up again, you can just keep the sonar going and it would tell you the exact depth of the sea bottom over your entire route of travel.

The first ship to make such use of sonar was German. It was the *Meteor*.

What happened was that a German chemist, Fritz Haber (HAH-ber, 1868–1934), had the idea that he might collect gold from sea water. He intended to use this to pay off the money demanded from Germany by the nations who had defeated her in World War I.

The *Meteor* was intended to test Haber's notions, and it set out to sea in 1922. It quickly showed, though, that the notion wouldn't work. There are indeed small quantities of gold dissolved in sea water, but it is so thinly spread out that it would take far more money to concentrate and collect it than the gold would be worth.

While at sea, however, the *Meteor* took sonar measurements of the sea bottom that began to revolutionize ideas about it.

Until then scientists had taken it for granted that the sea bottom was more or less flat, but the *Meteor* measurements showed that there are mountains rising up from the middle of the Atlantic Ocean. In fact, by 1925 the *Meteor* showed there is an entire mountain range winding down the Atlantic Ocean, longer and higher than any mountain ranges on the continents. It is called the Mid-Atlantic Ridge.

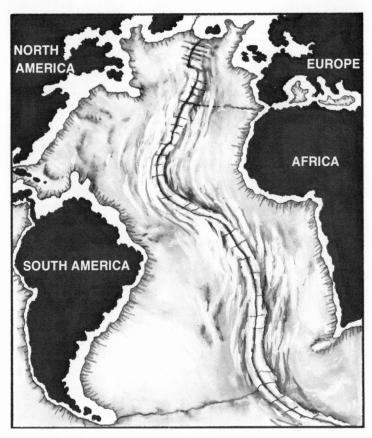

MID-ATLANTIC RIDGE

Later measurements of the sea depths by sonar showed that the Mid-Atlantic Ridge continues into other oceans, so that there is really a Mid-Oceanic Ridge.

What's more, just as the ocean has mountains that rise upward from the floor of the ocean, it also has "deeps" that are lower than the average floor of the ocean.

These deeps are not just holes in the ocean floor. They are curved regions called *trenches*, and they usually follow the lines of island chains near the boundaries of the ocean.

After World War II the ocean floor was examined in even more detail, and the exact depth of the various trenches was determined. Another ship called *Challenger* (in honor of Thomson's ship) discovered that the deepest regions in the ocean are in the western Pacific.

There the *Challenger* found a curve of deep water lying off the eastern shores of the Marianas Islands, which lie 1,500 miles east of the Philippines. The largest and southernmost of the Marianas Islands is Guam, which has been an American possession since 1898.

This curve of deep water is called the "Marianas Trench," and the deepest point in it

OCEAN FLOOR TOPOGRAPHY

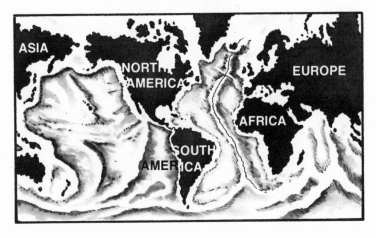

that the *Challenger* could find is now called
"Challenger Deep." It is located 250 miles
southwest of Guam and, in 1951, was shown to be
35,760 feet deep, or 6¾ miles. If Mount Everest,
the tallest mountain on Earth, were placed in
Challenger Deep, 1¼ miles of water would roll
over its peak.

In 1959, a Soviet ship, *Vityaz*, reported locating
a slightly deeper spot nearby that was 36,198 feet
down.

6 Men Beneath the Ocean

THE NEW knowledge of the ocean depths naturally raised questions as to whether living things were to be found even in the deepest trenches.

Ships were learning how to dredge up living animals from greater depths than ever. In 1947 a Swedish ship, *Albatross*, brought up animals from a depth of nearly 5 miles in the North Atlantic, and in 1952 a Danish ship, *Galathea*, brought up animals from a depth of more than 6 miles.

Such deep-sea animals did not survive long outside their native region. About the only way of learning about animals living under natural conditions in the deep sea would be to go down and look—but how?

Would it be possible to have underwater ships —a totally enclosed steel vessel capable of maneuvering under the ocean?

The first ships that could move about under water for at least a little while were built by a Dutchman named Cornelis van Drebbel (1572–1634) about 1620. He managed to maneuver his ship, made of wood and leather, about 12 feet under water. In 1801 the American inventor Robert Fulton (1765–1815), who later built the first practical steamship, built a submarine for Napoleon Bonaparte. He called it *Nautilus*, and it worked, but not well enough to suit Napoleon.

The difficulty was in maneuvering it. The logical way would be to use a steam engine to turn a propellor, but if you tried to burn fuel, you would quickly use up the air in the submarine.

In 1870 the science-fiction writer Jules Verne (1828–1905) wrote a very popular book, *Twenty Thousand Leagues under the Sea*, in which he imagined an advanced submarine he called *Nautilus*, after the one built by Robert Fulton. This spurred on inventors to keep on trying.

Finally, in 1886, a submarine (again named *Nautilus*) was built in Great Britain and was powered by electric batteries. This meant that the ship could be maneuvered well, but it had to come to the surface frequently in order to recharge its batteries. Still, it could travel 80 miles between rechargings.

By the time of World War I all the warring nations were using submarines.

After World War II attempts were made to build submarines that were powered by nuclear engines. Then there would be no need to surface and recharge batteries. Such *nuclear submarines* could stay under water for long times.

The first nuclear submarine was launched in 1955 by the United States. Again it was called *Nautilus*. The Soviet Union built its first nuclear submarine in 1959, and Great Britain built its first in 1963.

Nuclear submarines have cruised across the Arctic Ocean under the ice. Others have gone around the world without surfacing and have remained submerged for 3 months at a time.

Ordinary submarines have penetrated as much as 8,310 feet (1½ miles) below the surface, and some nuclear submarines can probably go considerably lower.

Meanwhile, other vessels specially designed for the deep sea came into being.

The first of these was used by the American naturalist Charles William Beebe (BEE-bee, 1877–1962).

U.S.S. *NAUTILUS*
FIRST NUCLEAR POWERED SUBMARINE

It was a hollow steel ball just large enough to hold two men. The walls were 1½ inches thick, and its interior was only 54 inches across. It weighed 2½ tons, and it could be lowered from its mother ship at the end of a steel cable. If, for any reason, the cable broke, that was the end. The steel ball would drop straight to the bottom and would not be recovered.

Beebe called it a *bathysphere* (BATH-ih-sfeer, or "ball of the deep").

In 1934 Beebe and a companion, Otis Barton, were lowered to a depth of 3,028 feet below the surface. Barton designed an even stronger bathysphere and descended to a record low of 4,500 feet ($^5/_6$ mile) in 1948. Through thick glass windows, in a beam of artificial light, animals could be seen living in their natural deep habitat.

**WILLIAM BEEBE,
OTIS BARTON,
AND BATHYSPHERE
AUGUST 11, 1930**

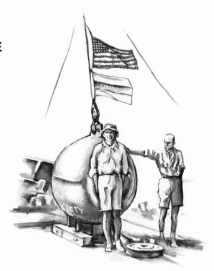

All together, more than thirty dives were made with bathyspheres, but what they could do was limited.

What was really needed was some vessel that could sink and rise again under its own power and that could reach the greatest possible depths.

Just this was in the mind of a Swiss scientist, Auguste Piccard (pee-KAHR, 1884–1962). Piccard in the early 1930s had used sealed gondolas suspended beneath large balloons to rise to record heights of nearly 10 miles into the upper atmosphere. All together, he made twenty seven balloon ascensions into the stratosphere.

In 1933, however, Piccard met Beebe at the Chicago World's Fair, and that started him thinking about exploration in the opposite direction —downward.

Instead of hanging a sealed cabin from a balloon capable of rising in the air, why not hang it from a balloon capable of rising in water? He began to design what he called a *bathyscaphe* (BATH-ih-skaf, or "ship of the deep").

The bathyscaphe consists of two parts. The upper part is a cigar-shaped float, containing thirteen tanks, eleven of which are filled with gasoline, and two of which are empty. Gasoline is lighter than water, and the entire float would tend to rise if it were submerged in water.

Tightly attached to the float is the bottom part, a bathysphere that holds human beings and instruments. The bathyscaphe is so designed that the float can just lift the weight of the bathysphere and keep it afloat.

The two empty tanks in the float can be opened and allowed to fill with sea water. The extra weight of the sea water drags down the bathyscaphe and causes it to sink into the ocean. It sinks downward to the very bottom of the sea.

If it is sinking too quickly, up to 13 tons of small iron pellets attached to the sphere can gradually be released. This makes the bathyscaphe lighter so that it sinks more slowly. If enough pellets are released, the bathyscaphe rises again, back to the surface.

Once the bathyscaphe has gone down and then returned to the surface, the sea water can be pumped out of the tanks and a new supply of iron pellets can be taken on so that it would be ready for another descent and ascent.

Piccard had to wait till after World War II before he could actually build his bathyscaphe. In 1948 the first one was completed. It was tested, rebuilt, and improved, and finally on February 15, 1954, in the first real test dive off the coast of west Africa, two French naval officers descended to a depth of 13,287 feet (2½ miles) and returned safely.

In 1953 a still better bathyscaphe was built, the *Trieste*, and in 1958 it was bought by the United States Navy. It was taken to California and was still further improved. Then it was ready for the big test.

**LIEUTENANT DON WALSH
AND JACQUES PICCARD
LEAVING THE *TRIESTE***

Out it went to the Marianas Trench. On board were Jacques Piccard (1922–), the son of Auguste, and an American naval officer, Don Walsh.

At 8:20 A.M. on January 23, 1960, the *Trieste* sank downward for 35,810 feet (6.8 miles) to the bottom of the trench and came to rest on soft mud. The mud billowed up and obscured the view for a while, but it slowly settled. As visibility got better, what the two men saw in their searchlights was a small red shrimp, about an inch long, floating by. They also saw a one-foot-long flounderlike fish.

There had been no doubt, really, but now at last there was clear eyewitness evidence that life existed at the very bottom of the sea.

The bathyscaphe then jettisoned iron pellets and rose to the surface. The two men were safely back at 5 P.M. after a very dangerous 13½-mile journey that took them 9 hours.

Have there been any real surprises waiting for people who penetrate into the deeper layers of the sea?

Yes, indeed. The earth's crust, we now know, is divided into plates,* and where the plates join, there can be weak places. In some places there are occasional *hot spots*, where heat from deep within the earth can work its way through the weak places into the ocean. The existence of such hot spots was first suspected in 1965, and in the early 1970s possible hot spots were detected by studying upward currents of warm water. (There would be up and down currents even without the hot spots, but the hot spots help.)

Beginning in 1977 a deep-sea submarine carried scientists downward to investigate the sea floor near hot spots east of the Galapagos Islands and at the mouth of the Gulf of California. In the latter hot spot they found *chimneys*, through which hot gushes of smoky mud surge upward, filling the surrounding sea water with minerals.

The minerals are rich in sulfur, and the neighborhood of these hot spots is full of special kinds of bacteria that obtain their energy from chemical reactions involving sulfur plus heat, instead of

*See *How Did We Find Out About Earthquakes?* (New York: Walker, 1978).

THE *TRIESTE*

from light. Small animals feed on these bacteria, and larger animals feed on the smaller ones.

This was a whole new chain of life forms that did not depend upon the plant cells in the surface of the sea. This chain can still exist even if there is no sunlight, provided heat and minerals continue to gush upward from the earth's interior. And, of course, they can exist only near the hot spots.

The scientists found clams, crabs, and various kinds of worms, some of them quite large. They are special species living in water filled with chemicals that are poisonous to other forms of life.

So, you see, there may still be a great deal left to learn about life in the deep sea.

TUBE WORMS NEAR GALAPAGOS ISLANDS

Index

61